THE TIMES

NATURE NOTES IIII

NATURE NOTES III

Peter Brookes

LITTLE, BROWN AND COMPANY

A *Little, Brown* Book

These 'Nature Notes' cartoons first published in *The Times* between July 1999 and June 2001
First published in this collection in Great Britain in 2001 by Little, Brown and Company

Copyright © 2001 by Peter Brookes and Times Newspapers, Ltd

The moral right of the author has been asserted.

ISBN: 0 316 858803

Printed and bound in Great Britain by Butler & Tanner Ltd, Frome and London

Little, Brown and Company (UK)
Brettenham House
Lancaster Place
London WC2E 7EN

For Angela, Benjamin and William

Computer problems cause long queues at passport offices; the 'integrated transport system' continues to crumble; Peter Mandelson's house loans controversy won't go away; the Tories are still the Tories…

Northern Ireland's peace process collapses when the Ulster Unionist Party makes Sinn Fein's admission to government conditional on IRA disarmament. Tony Blair is accused of being soft on terrorism.

NATURE NOTES

Taxidermy

Fig.1 Bag specimen

Fig.2 Render totally gutted

Fig. 3 Administer thorough stuffing

Fig. 4 Display

Air traffic control achieves agency status amid union fears that safety would be sacrificed to private profit. A Labour-dominated parliamentary committee attacks John Prescott's transport policy. In a reshuffle, Lord (Gus) Macdonald is made Transport Minister to assist the beleaguered Deputy Prime Minister.

NATURE NOTES

Fig.1
Treading water.

Fig.2
The high-flying gusmacdonald bird keeps a clean nose.

Unhappypotamus *(Transportintegratus disintegratus)*

For such a big beast, it has a surprisingly thin skin. A practised diver, it is all but submerged by its own bulk, barely keeping its head above muddied waters. Much persecuted; dangerous when wounded.

In the run-up to the Tory Conference in Blackpool a MORI poll puts Labour 27 points ahead. The Tories have failed to attract many of those dissatisfied with the government. Among this group William Hague's approval rating is now minus 45 points.

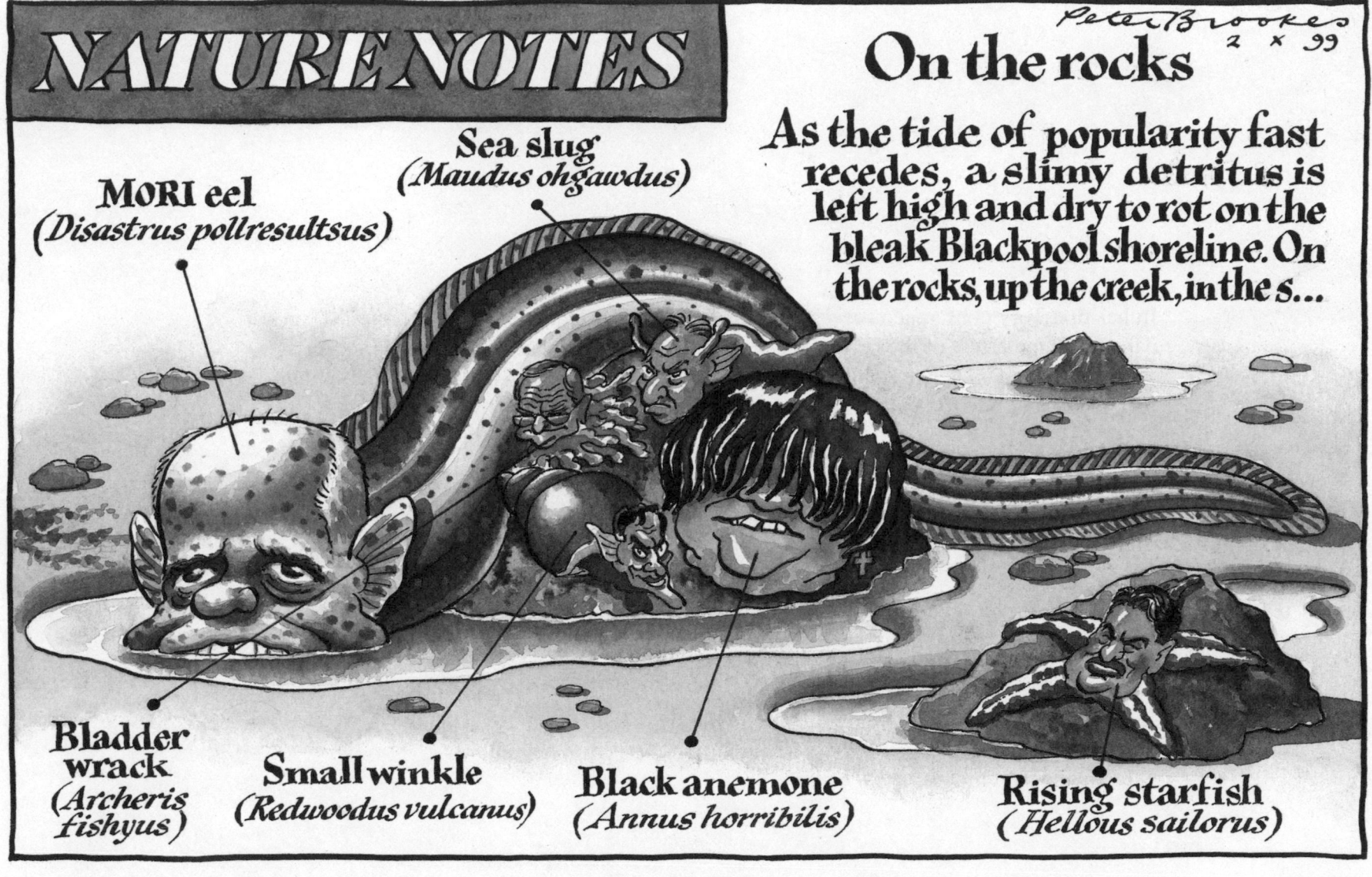

NATURE NOTES

On the rocks

Peter Brookes 2 × 99

As the tide of popularity fast recedes, a slimy detritus is left high and dry to rot on the bleak Blackpool shoreline. On the rocks, up the creek, in the s...

MORI eel
(Disastrus pollresultsus)

Sea slug
(Maudus ohgawdus)

Bladder wrack
(Archeris fishyus)

Small winkle
(Redwoodus vulcanus)

Black anemone
(Annus horribilis)

Rising starfish
(Hellous sailorus)

In her first Tory conference speech since she resigned as leader in 1990, Baroness Thatcher denounces the arrest of the reviled former Chilean dictator General Augusto Pinochet as 'judicial kidnap'. The adoring 800 Tory activists at Blackpool's ABC cinema stamp their feet, cheer and bay for Jack Straw's blood. William Hague is effectively sidelined.

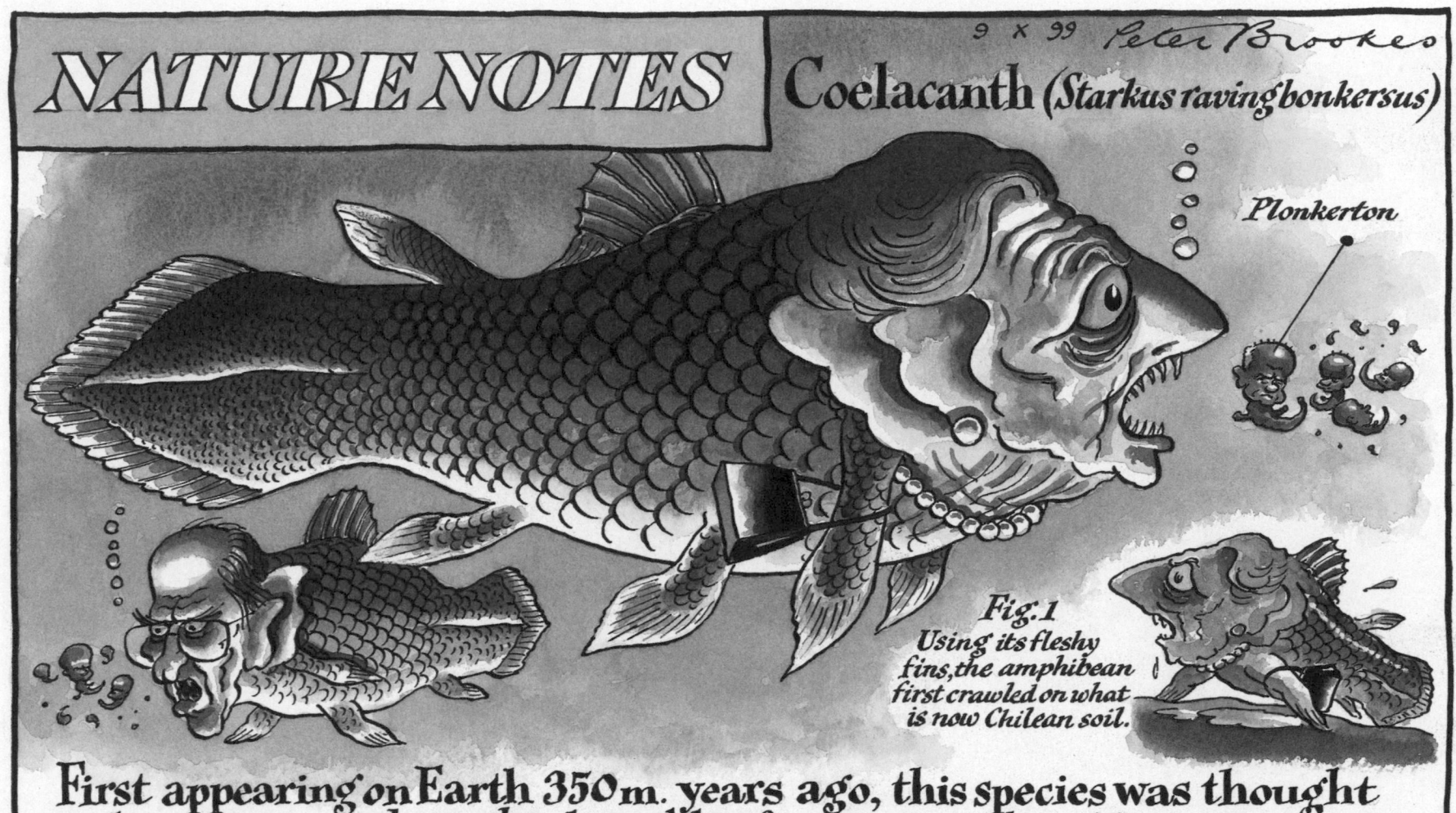

Threatened with expulsion from the party, left-wing Labour MP Ken Livingstone hints he would stand as an independent if prevented from becoming the official Labour nominee for London Mayor in a party stitch-up. The leadership unveils an electoral system designed to hinder Red Ken's chances of becoming the candidate, and to boost the prospects of Frank Dobson, the former Health Secretary.

NATURE NOTES

Fig 1 Pissed off as a newt.

Newt Labour
(Reddus kennus)

This winsome creature gains sympathy in its struggle against the tide of mean-minded party orthodoxy. But its own murky background might also slow progress. Getting to the top could be beyond our ken. Winsome, losesome.

BLAIR'S MAYOR

23 X 99

Peter Brookes

France refuses to drop its ban on British beef over fears of BSE. Nick Brown, Agriculture Minister, personally boycotts French produce but the Prime Minister, anxious to avoid a tit-for-tat trade war, refuses to say whether he backs him.

NATURE NOTES

Brown Cow
(Moomoo inthedoodoo)

Lumbering and bovine, but essentially placid, this prize *rosbif* takes a stand four-square in the *merde*. Like udders previously in its field, a complete and utter teat. Ripe for slaughter. How now, Brown cow?

The final task of the hereditary peers is to pass the House of Lords Reform Bill abolishing their seats. Their parting shot is a warning that Tony Blair could now adopt extensive powers of patronage.

Tony Blair is unexpectedly to become a father again with a fourth child due in May. Ken Livingstone could also become London Mayor that month, despite new Labour's 'control-freakery'.

NATURE NOTES

Stork *(Turnagainus livingstoneus)*
Traditionally a harbinger of unconfined joy and celebration, this myopic species can on occasion give new life to something a little less welcome. Bit of a cock-up all round.

20 xi 99
Peter Brookes

Michael Portillo returns to the front line of politics by comfortably winning the Kensington and Chelsea by-election, inevitably reopening speculation about William Hague's future as leader.

NATURE NOTES
Handling a new pet
(espec. Portillus caninus)
Do remember always to be vigilant and to be wary of extreme expressions of loyalty by your pooch.
Fig.1
Fig. 2
27 xi 99
Peter Brookes

John Prescott forces Railtrack to abandon its £2.5 billion bid to take over part of the London Underground in the aftermath of the Paddington disaster. Ken Livingstone, a fierce critic of the government's public-private partnership proposals, is delighted.

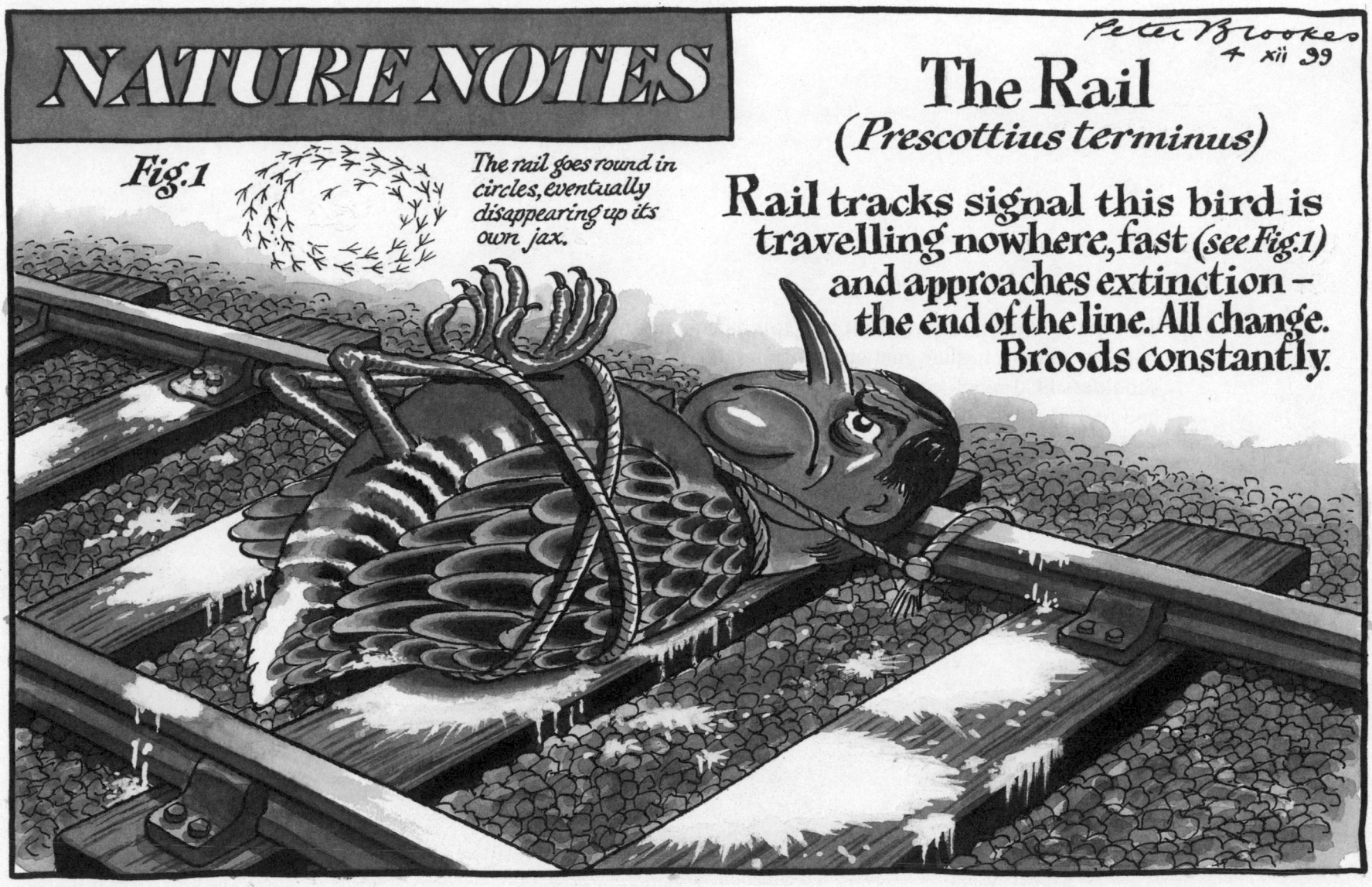

The Prime Minister reacts with fury to France's decision not to lift its ban on British beef imports without further guarantees of its safety. At the Helsinki EU summit Blair cold-shoulders his French counterpart and left-of-centre ally Lionel Jospin, angered by this 'wrong and regrettable decision'.

NATURE NOTES

Edible Frog
(Jospinus justdessertus)

For a truly satisfying alternative to beef follow this recipe for *Jospin à la Revenge*. First, catch the little slime-ball. Then, while it still draws breath, tear it limb from limb as it screams for mercy. Boil in oil. *Revenge* is a dish best eaten when cold.

TOPSIDE

A LOT OF NECK

SIRLOIN

RUMP

RIB

LEG

LEG

Fig. 1

Peter Brookes 11 xii 99

Jack Straw makes a spectacular U-turn in allowing boxer Mike Tyson to enter Britain in spite of his rape conviction. He cites fears that cancelling the £5 million fight at Manchester could cause business bankruptcies. Meanwhile he is 'minded' to release General Augusto Pinochet as being unfit to stand trial here.

Tony Blair reaches his one-thousandth day in office as Prime Minister.

NATURE NOTES — Flight

fig.1 fig.2 fig.3

After a thousand days most birds achieve sustained, if erratic, flight.

fig.1 fig.2 fig.3

And some were never meant to.

Peter Brookes 29 i 00

Rumours suggest that Frank Dobson has just scraped home in his bid to be Labour's candidate for mayor of London, amid left-wing accusations of a rigged selection procedure. The London Eye is a recent and highly popular addition to the skyline.

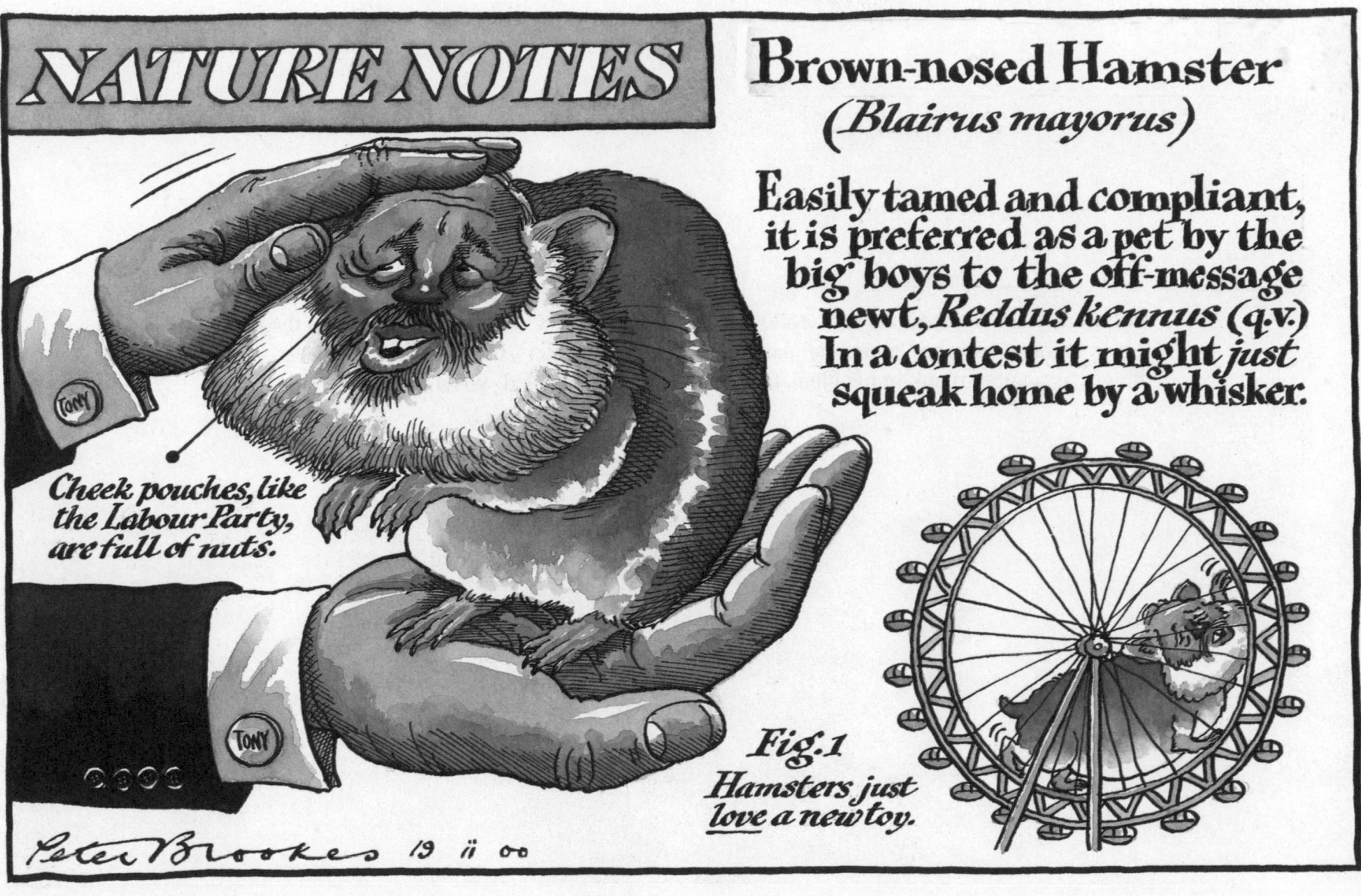

NATURE NOTES

Brown-nosed Hamster
(*Blairus mayorus*)

Easily tamed and compliant, it is preferred as a pet by the big boys to the off-message newt, *Reddus kennus* (q.v.) In a contest it might *just* squeak home by a whisker.

Cheek pouches, like the Labour Party, are full of nuts.

Fig. 1
Hamsters just <u>love</u> a new toy.

Peter Brookes 19 ii 00

Dobson is Labour candidate for London mayor. The defeated Livingstone condemns the election as 'tainted' and the Labour campaign as 'dead in the water', but Tony Blair sees the victory as another plank in his plans for devolved (but controlled) government.

NATURE NOTES

Theory of Devolution

26 ii 00 Peter Brookes

Once certain that devolution had happened, the unnaturalist 'Tony' Darwin propounded his view of unnatural selection in his tome *Origin of the Specious* (1859). This tract enthusiastically supported the idea of the survival of the least fit in the race for local supremacy. Fundamentalists and normal folk alike (particularly in London and Wales) were outraged at this insult to their *modus vivendi democratus*, but he denied he was attacking God's work because, after all, he *was* God.

Fig. 1 How species adapt

Before   After

Anthony Charles Lynton Darwin (1809-1882)

Barclays Bank closes well over a hundred rural branches with thousands due to shut across Britain in the next five years. With exquisite timing it emerges that the bank's new chief executive is in line for massive share options.

NATURE NOTES

The Fat Cat
(Bonus obscenus)

Laws of physics dictate that stupid fat cats remove branches at their peril. You can bank on it *(see Fig.1),* with interest.

Fig.1

A complete bunch of bankers.

The race for London mayor is almost run. Competing are Ken Livingstone (Independent), Steve Norris (Conservative), Frank Dobson (Labour) and Susan Kramer (Liberal Democrat).

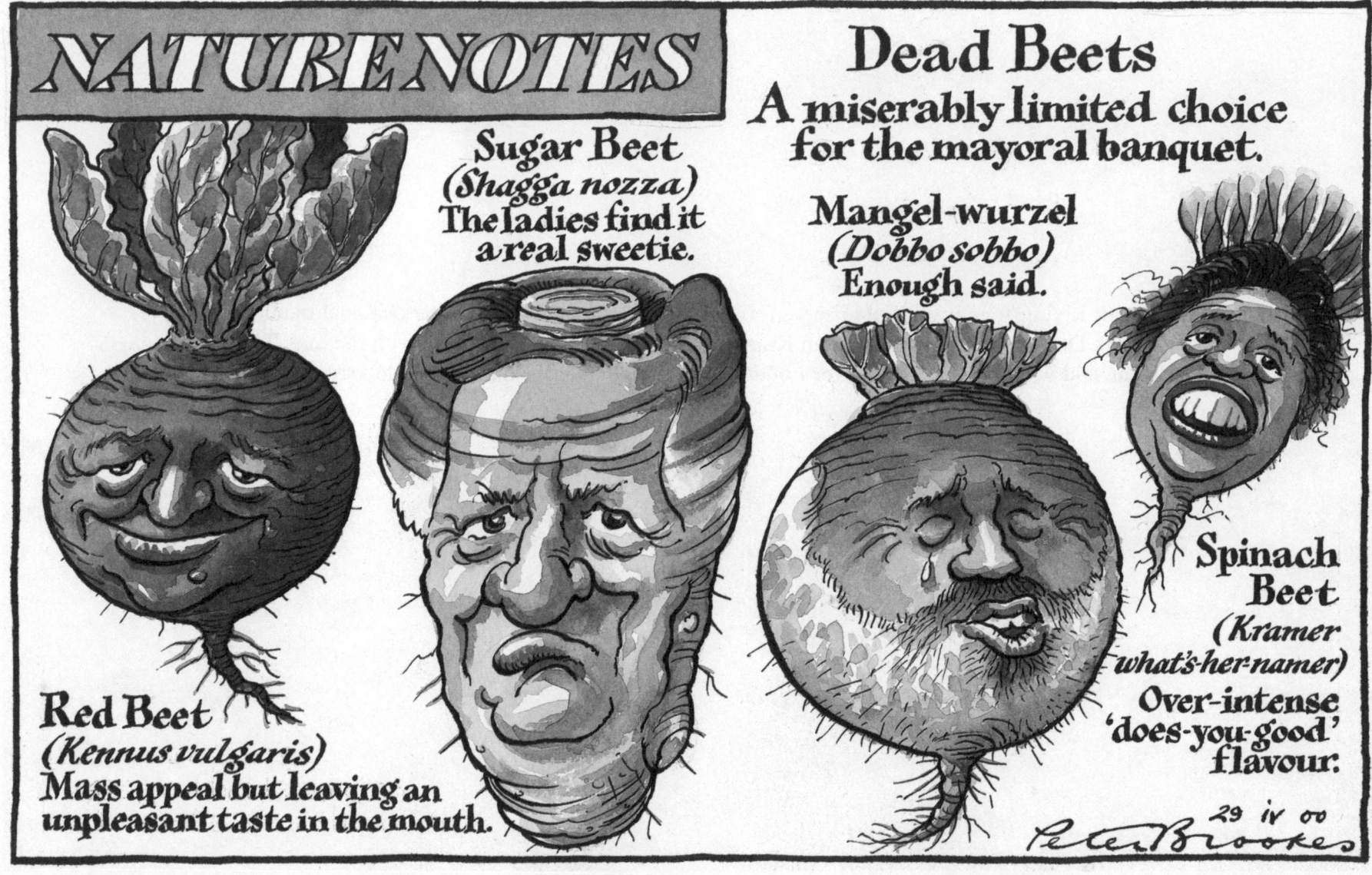

NATURE NOTES

Sugar Beet
(Shagga nozza)
The ladies find it
a real sweetie.

Red Beet
(Kennus vulgaris)
Mass appeal but leaving an
unpleasant taste in the mouth.

Dead Beets
A miserably limited choice
for the mayoral banquet.

Mangel-wurzel
(Dobbo sobbo)
Enough said.

**Spinach
Beet**
*(Kramer
what's-her-namer)*
Over-intense
'does-you-good'
flavour.

29 iv 00
Peter Brookes

Mayor Livingstone is elected to serve for four years with an overwhelming personal mandate (Frank Dobson only just pips Susan Kramer to third place). Confrontation with the man Tony Blair said would be a 'disaster' for London seems inevitable for the Labour leadership.

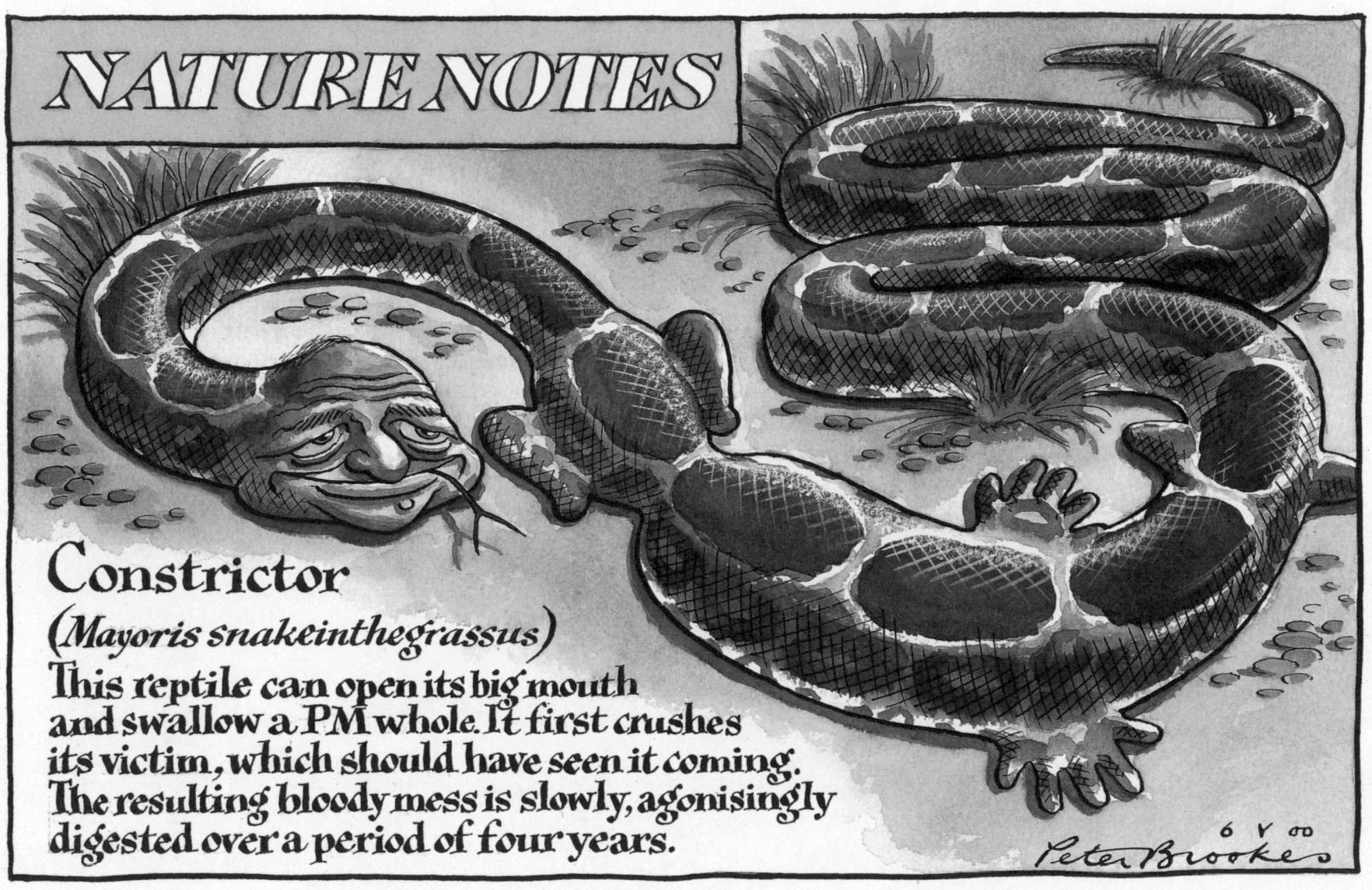

NATURE NOTES

Constrictor
(*Mayoris snakeinthegrassus*)

This reptile can open its big mouth
and swallow a PM whole. It first crushes
its victim, which should have seen it coming.
The resulting bloody mess is slowly, agonisingly
digested over a period of four years.

British forces are scheduled to extend their stay in Sierra Leone amid concerns that they could be sucked into the civil war (so-called 'mission creep'). Foreign Secretary Robin Cook adds to the confusion. 'When I say they will not be combat troops, I do not want any misunderstanding by the rebels that these people cannot hit back and cannot hit back hard if they are attacked.'

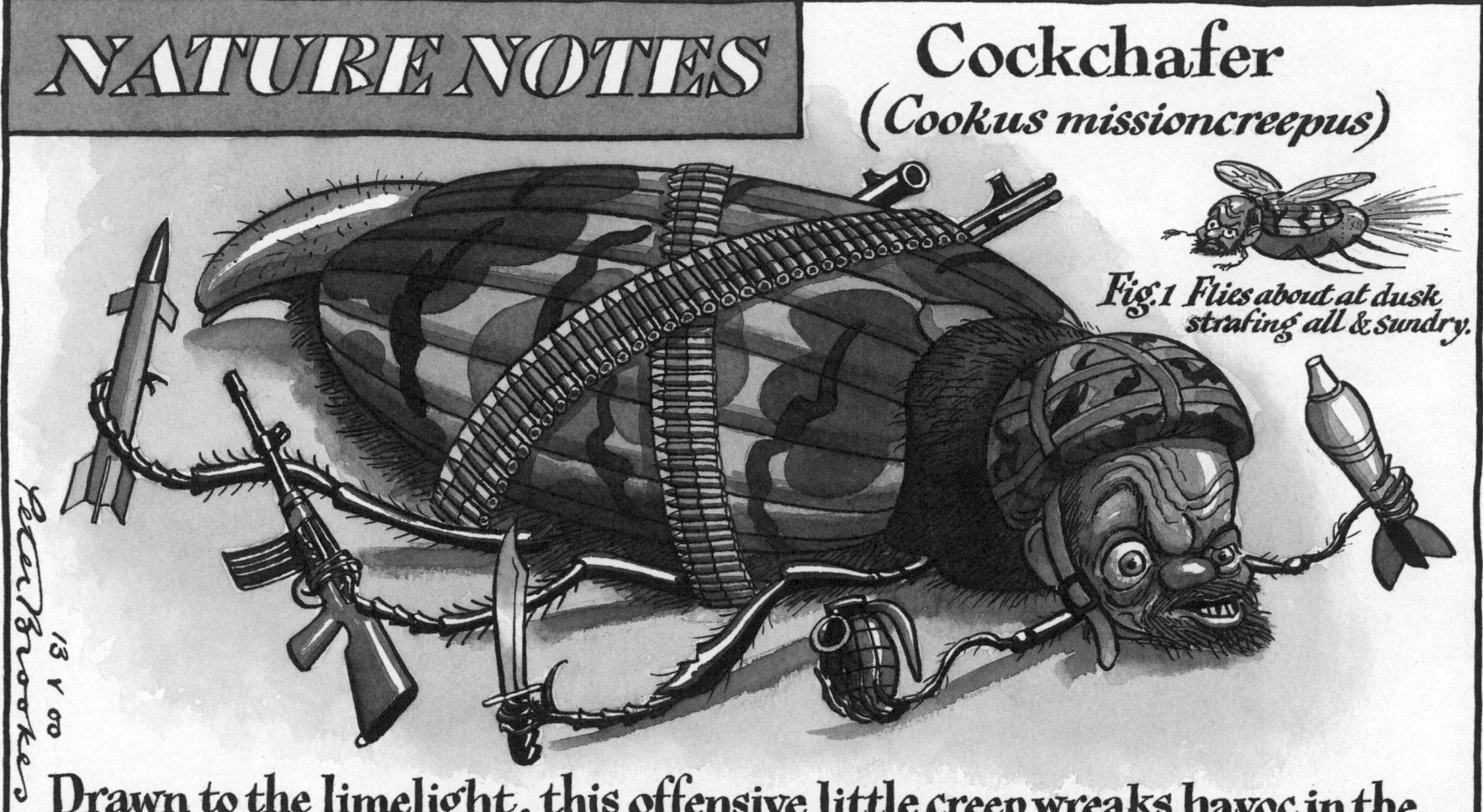

NATURE NOTES

Cockchafer
(Cookus missioncreepus)

Fig.1 Flies about at dusk strafing all & sundry.

Drawn to the limelight, this offensive little creep wreaks havoc in the jungles of Sierra Leone and East Timor, the Balkan uplands and the Iraqi desert. Is sucked inexorably into a mire of its own making.

Tony Blair, who assumes they will eat out of his hand, is heckled by 10,000 W.I. members at Wembley Arena. Meanwhile, the fox-hunting debate intensifies. The Duke of Edinburgh maintains that the introduction of the grey squirrel from abroad has done far more harm to the environment than GM crops ever have. This puts him directly at odds with his son, the Prince of Wales, a bitter opponent of GM experimentation.

Tony Blair is attacked by his one-time mentor, Lord Jenkins of Hillhead, Chancellor of Oxford university. Gordon Brown had criticised Oxford for rejecting Laura Spence, a comprehensive school candidate hoping to read Medicine. Bon viveur Jenkins is still smarting from his proportional representation proposals having been sidelined by Blair, who commissioned them.

NATURE NOTES

A Good Whine
Essential tasting notes

1982

VINEYARD 'MAGDALEN'

Chateau Woy

CRU BOURGEOIS

APPELLATION DEGREE HONORAIRE CONTRÔLÉE

12% vol.   PRODUIT D'OXFORD   75cl

MISE TOUT EN BOUTEILLE AU CHATEAU

Fig.1 Dégustation

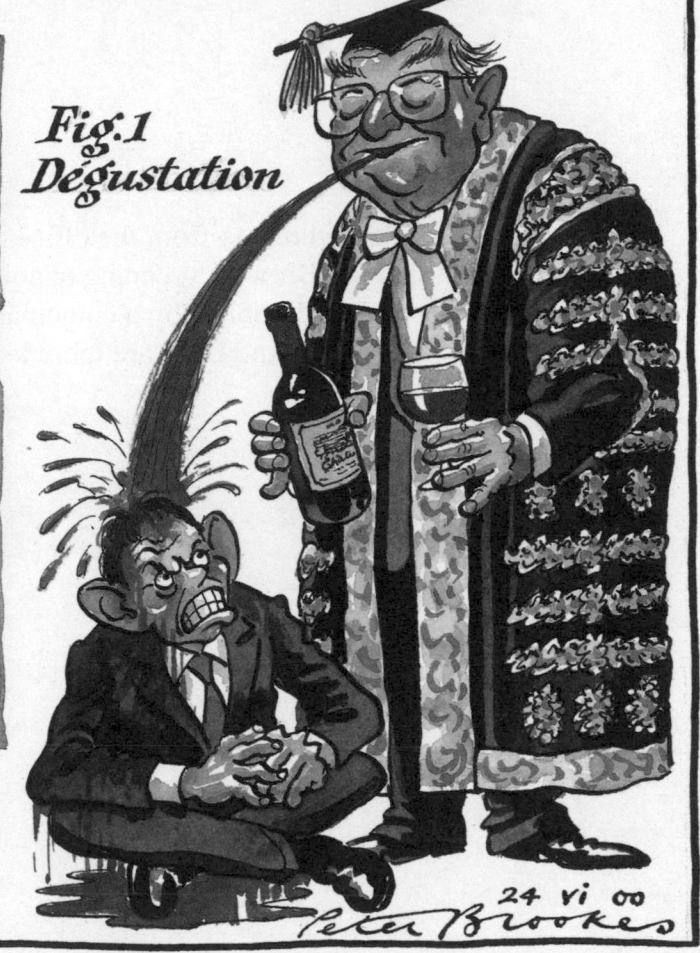

A substantial, if not *élite*, property run by the *awiviste* Woy family. The wine is now severe and acidic in style, a product of sour grapes.

24 vi oo
Peter Brookes

A leaked memo from the office of Philip Gould, Tony Blair's polling guru, threatens to derail Gordon Brown's spending announcement. In his memo Gould says that the government has been 'undermined by a combination of spin, lack of conviction, and apparent lack of integrity'. And there are more leaks to come.

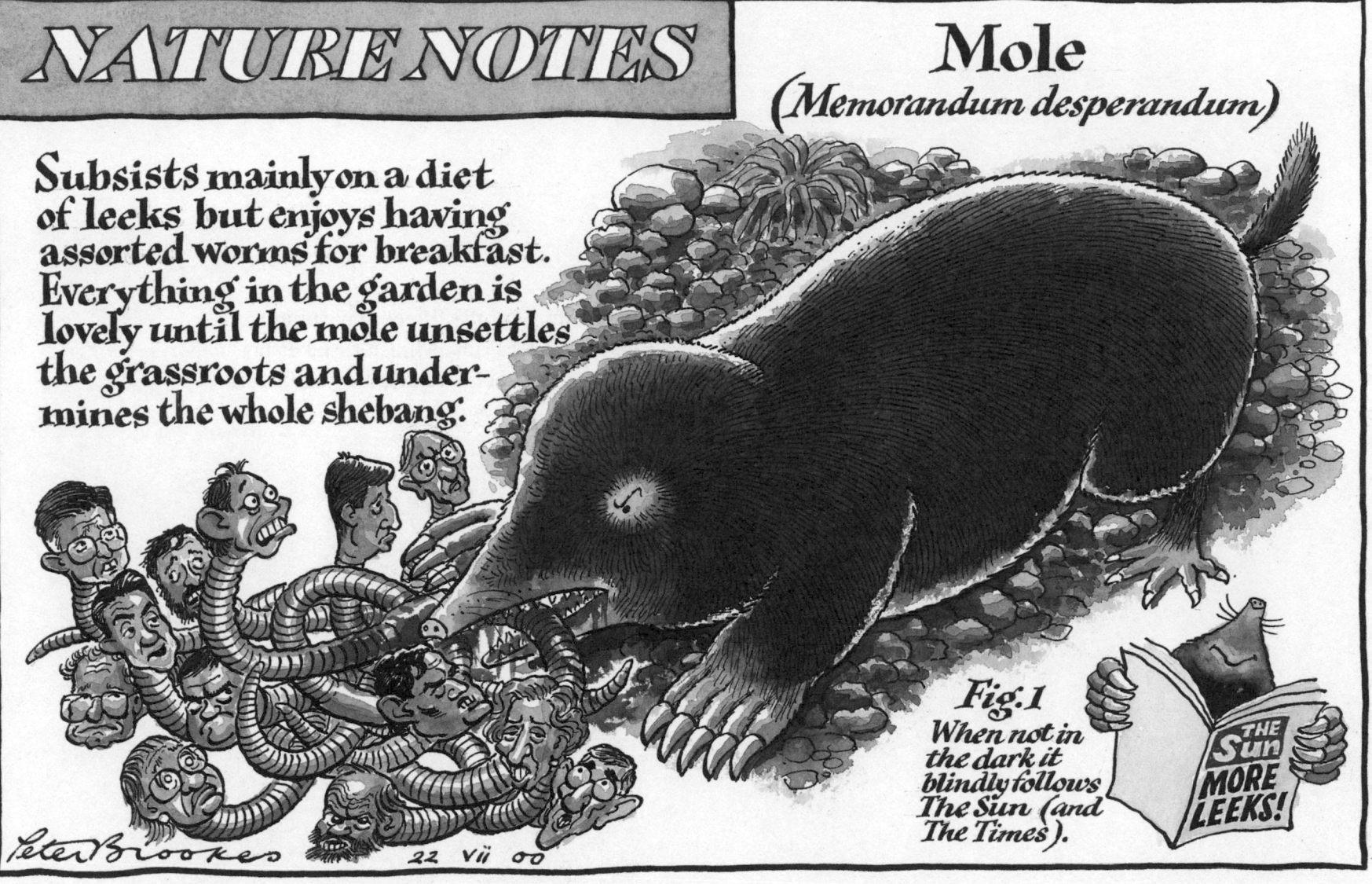

NATURE NOTES

Mole
(*Memorandum desperandum*)

Subsists mainly on a diet of leeks but enjoys having assorted worms for breakfast. Everything in the garden is lovely until the mole unsettles the grassroots and under-mines the whole shebang.

Fig. 1
When not in the dark it blindly follows The Sun (and The Times).

THE Sun
MORE LEEKS!

Peter Brookes   22 vii 00

The inability to agree on the future of Jerusalem spells failure for the fifteen-day summit at Camp David, hosted by President Clinton. Ehud Barak, Israel's Prime Minister, stakes his political future in ceding parts of Jerusalem to the Palestinians, but is rejected by an obdurate Yasser Arafat.

NATURE NOTES

Shit of the Desert *(Yasser irrascibilis)*
Bites and spits when it gets the double hump, giving no one any
peace. Well-nigh useless, but at least its dried dung makes good fuel.

The Russian submarine *Kursk* sinks in the Barents Sea and all 118 crew perish. President Putin is slow to return from holiday and the bad old communist days are echoed in the ensuing disinformation and quashing of dissent (film footage of a bizarre sedation by injection of the protesting mother of one of the dead sailors).

NATURE NOTES

Coldfish
(Putinus pusillanimous)

Although this coldfish has no discernible warmth, it prefers the shallows of holiday beaches to the icy arctic depths. It is often to be found around The Needles.

Conning tower

Conning bastard

Fig. 1 Beware: these bones can stick in the craw.

26 viii oo

Peter Brookes

Dome Minister Lord Falconer of Thoroton presides over yet another call on lottery funds to bail out the troubled millennium attraction and prevent its early closure. An extra £47 million is ploughed in, taking to £244 million the additional payments made in the past year. All on top of the £400 million lottery grant it took to build it in the first place. Lord Falconer, a lawyer, has no previous experience in running an entertainments complex.

Petrol is predicted to hit £4 a gallon by the end of the year and farmers, hauliers, and taxi-drivers blockade the refineries in protest. Troops are put on standby as the health service goes on emergency alert, schools and businesses close and supermarkets introduce rationing. The government is very slow to react to panic buying at the pumps and as Britain runs out of fuel, the government runs of out ideas to solve the crisis.

NATURE NOTES

Storm Petrol
(Pumpus chumpus)

This harbinger of stormy weather is the rarest of visitors to rural habitats, preferring to be all at sea. When freezing in a winter of public discontent, it will opt for a novel method of keeping warm. This it deems a success.

Fig.1

16 ix 00

Peter Brookes

Do not try this at home.

The bird is adept at skimming surfaces

Clare Short, International Development Secretary, strays 'off message' on BBC1's *Question Time* and admits that the Millennium Dome was a 'disaster' that should never have been built.

NATURE NOTES

Hoary Old Chestnut
(Domeus badjokeus)

Fig.1   Nut case

Fig.2 Knock it

Fig.3 Stoop to conker

Fig: 4 Thwak!

In a referendum Denmark say 'Nej' to the euro by a margin of 53 per cent to 47. It is a huge blow to Denmark's entire political, corporate, and media establishment, and to Tony Blair's (and Robin Cook's and Peter Mandelson's) ambition to take Britain into the euro in the next parliament. At a stroke the idea that membership is inevitable is destroyed.

NATURE NOTES

Great Dane
(Euro urineus)

Truculent breed which refuses to do its master's bidding and happily soils the neighbour's patch. Cocks a snook at established opinion. There's a good boy.

Fig. 1 Excellent manure

The closest election in US history hangs on the delayed Florida result. Bush has won 29 states for 246 electoral college votes. Gore has won 19 states plus the District of Columbia for 260. Florida, with 25 votes, is being recounted. The lawyers move in. A total vote of 48,976,148 for Gore as against 48,783,510 for Bush (so far) means there is everything to play for in the Sunshine State.

Meanwhile, Hillary Clinton triumphs in New York and is already considered a possible runner in 2004, the other Clinton presidency a fading memory. The Florida count, recount and re-recount continues, with its myriad forms of machine-ballot 'chad' creating more heat than light.

NATURE NOTES

Birds of America
Your cut-out & keep guide to the high-flyers

Peter Brookes
25 xi 00

Cuckoo (*Uxor hillaryius*)
Parasitic female which invades other nests. Likes big apple trees.

Hornbill (*Preposterus proboscis*)
Definitely has an eye for the birds. Often flies undone.

Electoral College Turkey
(*Electus decrepitus*)
Past its sell-by date and hard to swallow. Ready for the chop.

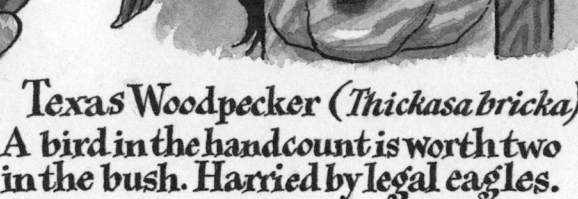

Texas Woodpecker (*Thickasa bricka*)
A bird in the handcount is worth two in the bush. Harried by legal eagles.

Fig. 1
Pregnant (or Nipple) Chadfinch

Fig. 2
Hanging Chadfinch

Fig. 3
Swinging Chadfinch

ME FOR 2004

The forthcoming EU Summit in Nice spells trouble, with Britain isolated over the tax veto. Tensions have already been heightened by John Prescott's 'macho' behaviour towards his French opposite number, Environment Minister Dominique Voynet, at climate change talks. William Hague has famously declared he downed fourteen pints in one day as a young man.

NATURE NOTES

Pond Life of Europe
A guide to the depths of Anglo-French understanding:

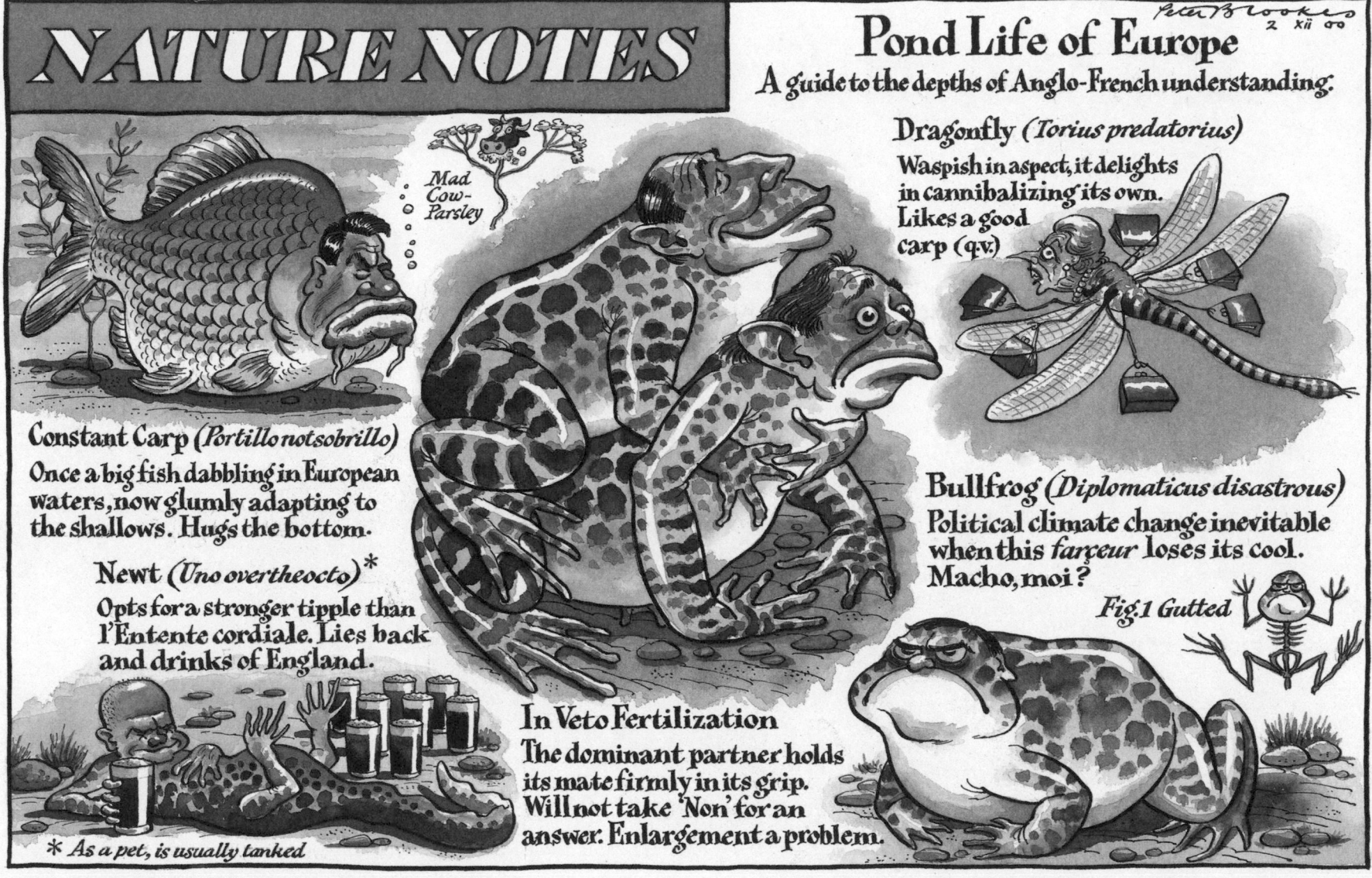

Mad Cow-Parsley

Constant Carp (*Portillo notsobrillo*)
Once a big fish dabbling in European waters, now glumly adapting to the shallows. Hugs the bottom.

Newt (*Uno overtheocto*) *
Opts for a stronger tipple than l'Entente cordiale. Lies back and drinks of England.

* *As a pet, is usually tanked*

In Veto Fertilization
The dominant partner holds its mate firmly in its grip. Will not take 'Non' for an answer. Enlargement a problem.

Dragonfly (*Torius predatorius*)
Waspish in aspect, it delights in cannibalizing its own. Likes a good carp (q.v.)

Bullfrog (*Diplomaticus disastrous*)
Political climate change inevitable when this *farçeur* loses its cool. Macho, moi?

Fig.1 Gutted

Lord Lamont of Lerwick is awarded an Augusto Pinochet Foundation 'Star of Merit' at a ceremony in Santiago for his work in defence of the former Chilean dictator.

Al Gore finally concedes and George W. Bush is America's 43rd President, ending five weeks of bitter wrangling.

NATURE NOTES

Beating about the Bush
Your guide to the changing political landscape.

Republican Elephant
(Dumbo jumbo)
Big beast, small brain.

Dickpicker
(Cheneyus veepus)
Keeps its master clean.

Fig. 1
Electric howdah

Trunk is used for hard drinking and snorting.

Democrat Donkey
(Goreus boreus)
Bit of an ass. Will never run again.

Barbara Bush   George Bush   Laura Bush   Jeb Bush   'Spot' Bush

Butterfly Ballot

16 xii 00

Peter Brookes

Jack Straw revives the hopes of foxhunters by backing the Middle Way Group which proposes allowing hunting as a licensed activity following strict codes of practice. Ironically a Labour Home Secretary is now seen to be supporting hunting while his Conservative Shadow, Ann Widdecombe, is in favour of a ban.

NATURE NOTES

Hurrah for the Berkeley Hunt!
How to ingratiate yourself with the Countryside Lobby.

Fig.1 Brown nose with the Utter-B'stards!

Fig.2 Exult in the excitement of the chase!

Fig. 3 Thrill to the kill!

Peter Brookes 28 xii 00

With the new year, election fever mounts. Defence Secretary Geoff Hoon rebuts an army medical report which warned of the high risk of cancer faced by soldiers who handled Iraqi tanks hit by depleted uranium shells in the Gulf War. The MOD is accused by veterans of a cover-up.

A Libyan intelligence agent gets twenty years for killing the 270 victims of the Lockerbie bombing, prompting immediate demands for retribution against Colonel Gaddafi's regime from the victims' relatives.

Following a second forced resignation (over the Hinduja passport affair) Peter Mandelson mounts a furious fight-back, bitter over the role of the Home Office in his dismissal. This in turn angers the Blair team by deflecting press attention away from the Prime Minister's major speech on his second-term objectives.

NATURE NOTES

Kangaroo Court
(*Marsupialis inthesoupialis*)

Adept at boxing clever, the infant marsupial fights back with a vengeance after being summarily told to hop it, causing not inconsiderable damage. Its parent may well roo the day.

Fig.1 It will rely on a convoluted tale to achieve balance as it bounces back.

It's no picnic at Hanging Rock.

Casus campbelli

The Legacy deal to create a dot.com venture park at the redundant Millennium Dome site in Greenwich collapses. Pierre-Yves Gerbeau, the Dome's former chief executive, is now back in the running to make a bid.

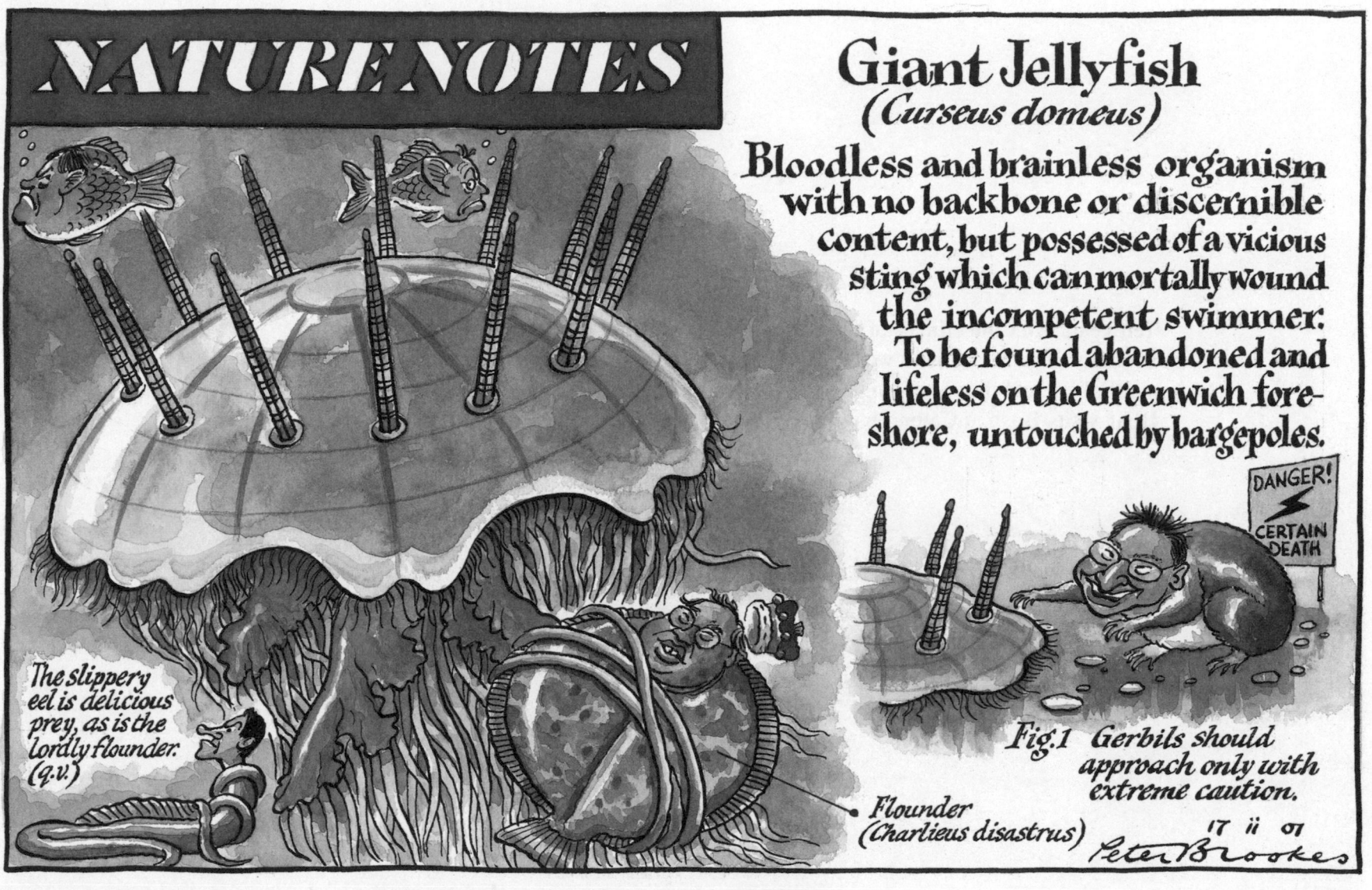

NATURE NOTES

Giant Jellyfish
(Curseus domeus)

Bloodless and brainless organism with no backbone or discernible content, but possessed of a vicious sting which can mortally wound the incompetent swimmer: To be found abandoned and lifeless on the Greenwich fore-shore, untouched by bargepoles.

The slippery eel is delicious prey, as is the lordly flounder. (q.v.)

DANGER! CERTAIN DEATH

Fig.1 Gerbils should approach only with extreme caution.

Flounder *(Charlieus disastrus)*

17 ii 01

Peter Brookes

Ten years after the climax of Operation Desert Storm, President Bush and his team of veterans from his father's war unleash American firepower on Baghdad in an act of echoing symbolism and dynastic vengeance. As always, Britain tags along, a position confirmed when Blair visits Bush at Camp David for bonding sessions.

NATURE NOTES

Gorilla Warfare

Peter Brookes
24 ii 07

Emerging from their bush habitat onto desert terrain, the *Gorilla imperator* and its hanger-on engage in bonding exercises. Lethal missiles are launched indiscriminately with no regard for innocent life or limb. A dangerous bunch of nutters.

A pig of a week as foot-and-mouth disease spreads from a Northumberland farm, putting large areas of rural Britain out of bounds to visitors. Farmers give Nick Brown a roasting and there's a butchering for other ministers too.

Sir Anthony Hammond's inquiry into the Hinduja passport affair formally clears both Peter Mandelson and Keith Vaz, the Foreign Office Minister, of any impropriety.

Lord Irvine of Lairg, Lord Chancellor, attempts to raise funds from Labour lawyers; Keith Vaz stonewalls parliament's standards watchdog Elizabeth Filkin; Jack Straw undermines Peter Mandelson; Robin Cook denies lying to the House over arms-to-Africa; Tony Blair presides.

NATURE NOTES

Asparrogance
(Neverus questionus)

At bottom it affects a whiter than whiteness while displaying a sleazy hue at the tips. When brought to table smothered in buttery unction, it positively oozes goodness. It is pronounced almost without blemish by top TV chefs Delia Filkin and Ainsley 'Wally' Hammond, and a pathetically grateful nation just laps it up (cf. rhubarb).

Fig.1 A greasy spear is grasped with two fingers, thus.

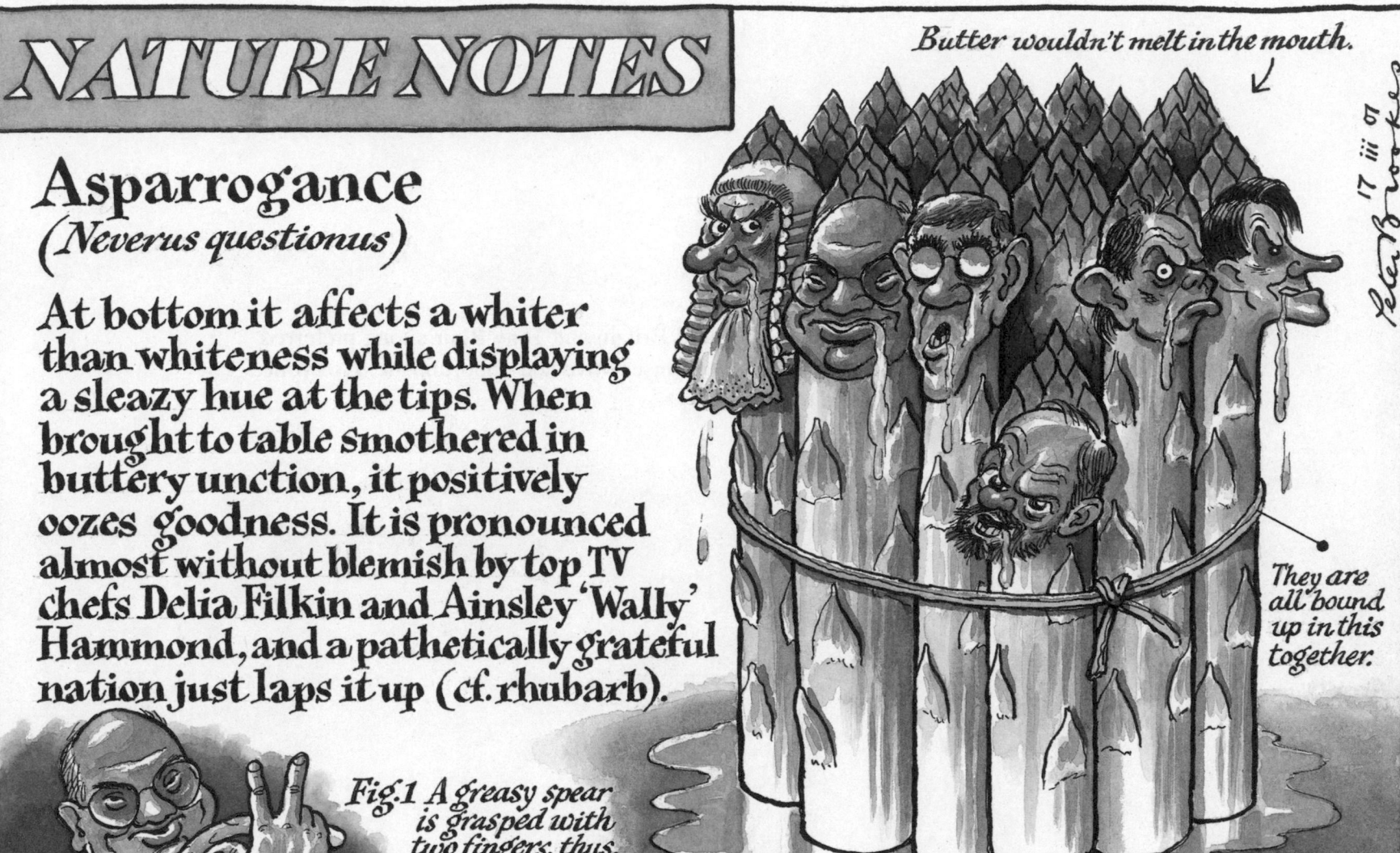

Butter wouldn't melt in the mouth.

They are all bound up in this together.

Foot-and-mouth disease continues to ravage rural Britain and Tony Blair's long preferred date of 3 May for the general election now looks insensitive and opportunistic. Everyone, including senior bishops, pitches in to urge delay.

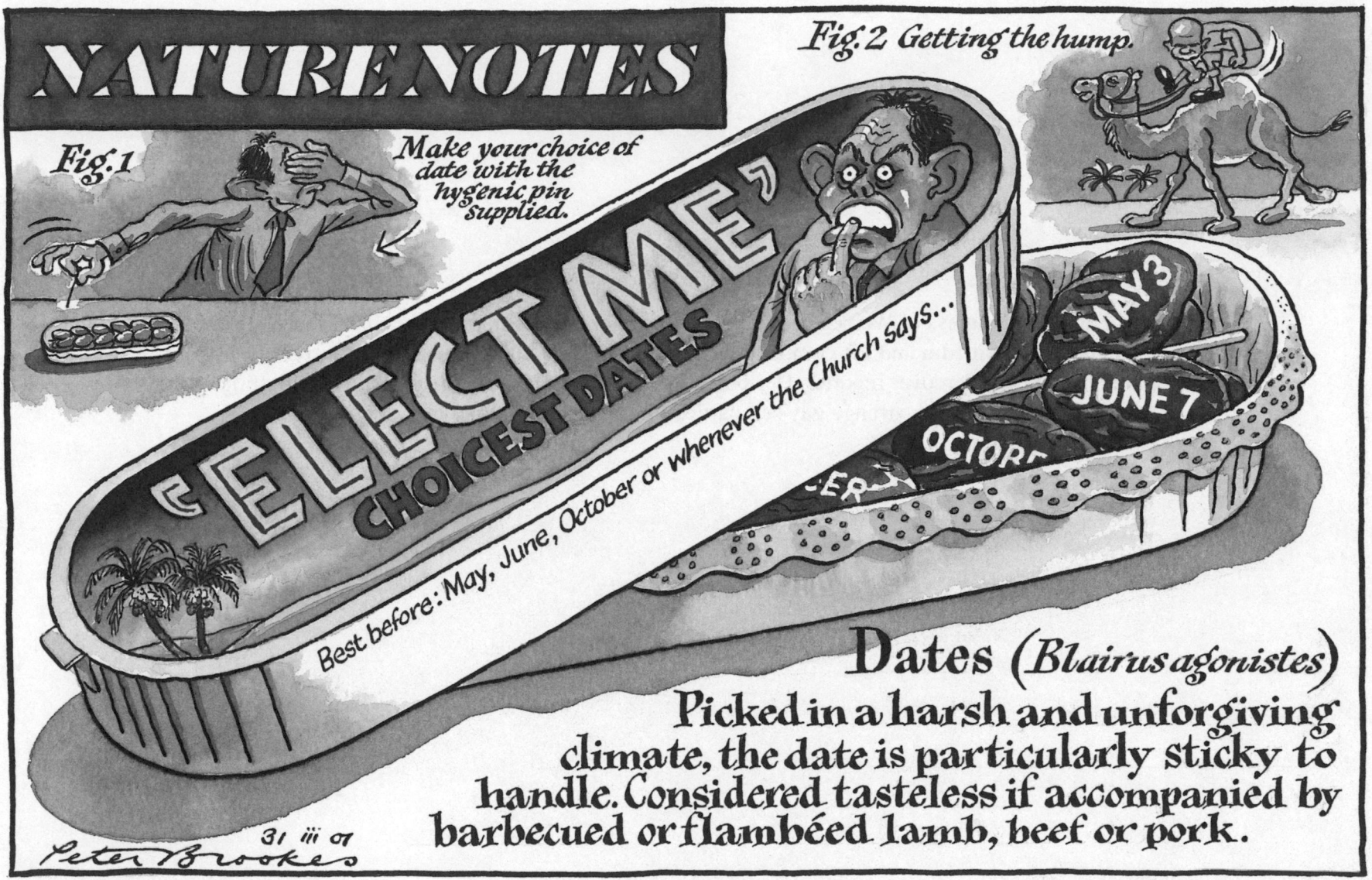

NATURE NOTES

Fig. 1

Make your choice of date with the hygenic pin supplied.

Fig. 2 Getting the hump.

"ELECT ME"
CHOICEST DATES

Best before: May, June, October or whenever the Church says...

MAY 3

JUNE 7

OCTOBER

Dates (*Blairus agonistes*)
Picked in a harsh and unforgiving climate, the date is particularly sticky to handle. Considered tasteless if accompanied by barbecued or flambéed lamb, beef or pork.

31 iii 01

Peter Brookes

The Earl and Countess of Wessex are deemed to have exploited their royal name for profit, to the benefit of their film and PR companies. She is duped into highly-quotable indiscretions by a 'fake sheikh' undercover reporter. Her business partner resigns after he was taped admitting taking drugs, offering to arrange gay sex parties for clients and calling into doubt the Earl's sexuality. A right royal mess.

NATURE NOTES

Wessex Saddleback Pair
(Horridus horridus horridus)
They engorge on an unsavoury swill mix of business and royal privilege by pushing their greedy snouts in the trough. Too prone to foot-in-mouth.

Fig.1 Related to the organically farmed Gloucester Old Spot.

Easter approaches, as does the general election.

Charles Kennedy has not performed particularly well in the House as Lib Dem leader, and is considered a 'soft touch' for both Tony Blair and William Hague. (How wrong can you be? He was to have a highly successful general election campaign.)

The Prime Minister is set to call a general election…

Only a month to go before some very familiar and long-established figures retire from the House of Commons, in some cases to reappear in the House of Lords (as Lady Thatcher already has done, of course).

The election campaign is in full swing as is the Deputy Prime Minister's fist. He punches an egg-throwing protester but is, on balance, lauded for it. The Tories wheel out the Baroness, thereby sidelining their nominal leader Hague. Ann Widdecombe, Shadow Home Secretary would herd up any asylum-seeker that moved and Tony Blair reveals his patriotic credentials.

The Tories, predictably, are struggling and already the knives are out.

Blair storms back to No.10 with a 167 majority, a second and historic landslide. Hague resigns; Portillo disappears to Morocco, to spend time in contemplation; Mandelson makes a bizarre, bitter and crazed acceptance speech; the Man in The White Suit is skewered; Kennedy takes off.

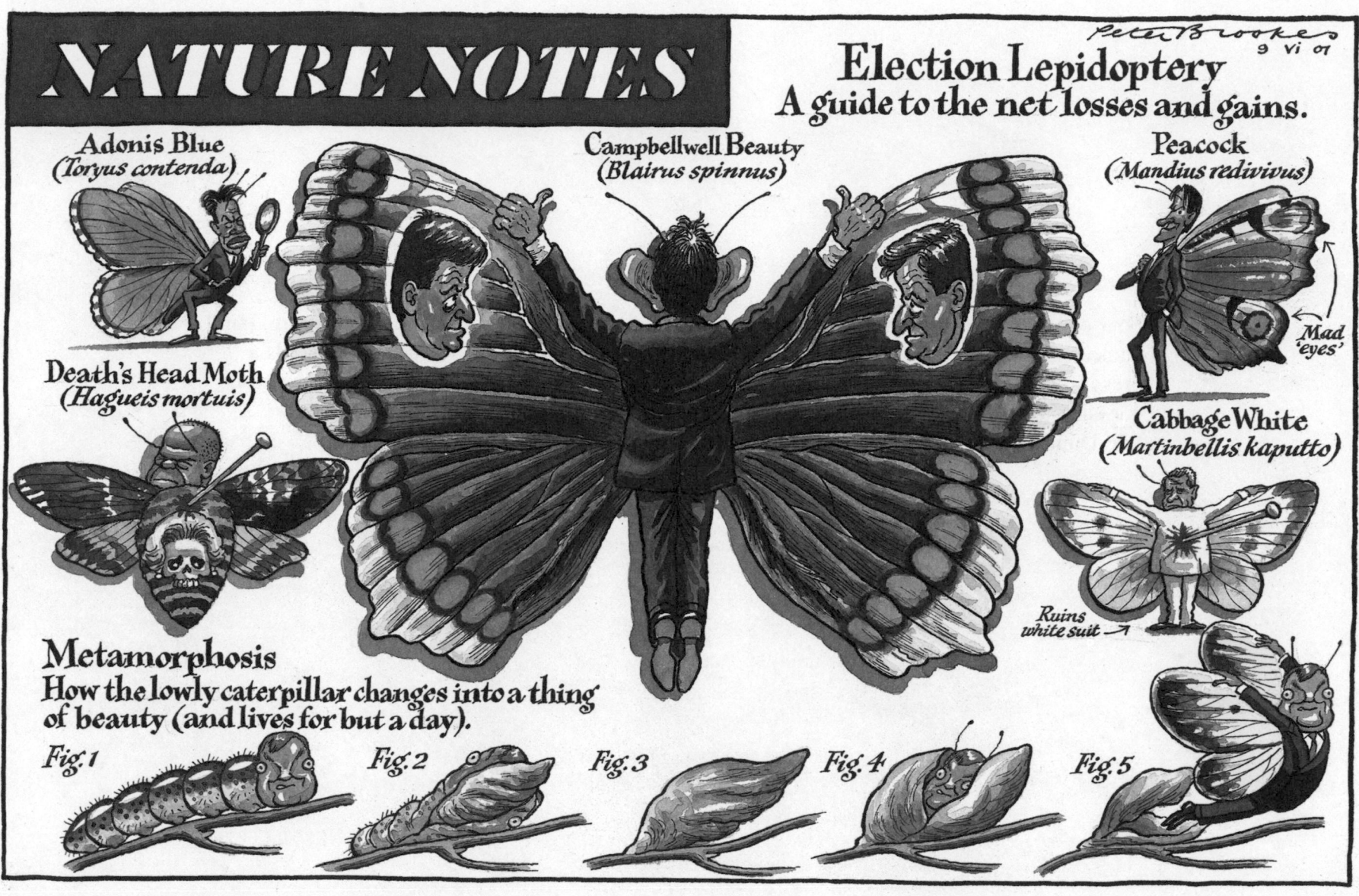

NATURE NOTES

Election Lepidoptery
A guide to the net losses and gains.

Adonis Blue
(Toryus contenda)

Campbellwell Beauty
(Blairus spinnus)

Peacock
(Mandius redivivus)

Mad 'eyes'

Death's Head Moth
(Hagueis mortuis)

Cabbage White
(Martinbellis kaputto)

Ruins white suit →

Metamorphosis
How the lowly caterpillar changes into a thing of beauty (and lives for but a day).

Fig. 1   Fig. 2   Fig. 3   Fig. 4   Fig 5

Four candidates for the vacant Tory leadership put themselves forward (Michael Ancram, Iain Duncan Smith, Michael Portillo and David Davis). A fifth Tory, Ann Widdecombe, holds a press conference to announce her non-candidacy and a sixth, Kenneth Clarke, keeps everyone guessing as to whether he will stand or not. He does. But later it is Kenneth Clarke and Iain Duncan Smith who go through to the ballot of the membership as a whole.

NATURE NOTES

Tory Tits

Peter Brookes
23 · vi · 01

Crested Tit
(Ancramus toffus)
Tit of the highest order. Seeks out the centre ground.

Blot on escutcheon

Tommy Tit
(Duncus smithus)
By the loony right, quick march!

Blue-breasted Tit
(Widdecombea backbitea)
High-flyer brought to earth. Lacks sufficient support.

PROPERTY OF BRITISH AMERICAN TOBACCO

Coal-tar Tit
(Clarkeus europeus)
A late arrival from Vietnam to the killing fields of Westminster.

Tall-tale Tit
(Portillus touchifeelius)
Visits the wilder shores. Will fly upside down for a lark.

NB Davidus davisus is very rarely sighted.

NATURE NOTES — Tory Tits

Peter Brookes 23 · VI · 01

Crested Tit (*Ancramus toffus*) Tit of the highest order. Seeks out the centre ground.

Blot on escutcheon

Tommy Tit (*Duncus smithus*) By the loony right, quick march!

PROPERTY OF BRITISH AMERICAN TOBACCO

Blue-breasted Tit (*Widdecombea backbitea*) High-flyer brought to earth. Lacks sufficient support.

Coal-tar Tit (*Clarkeus europeus*) A late arrival from Vietnam to the killing fields of Westminster.

Tall-tale Tit (*Portillus touchifeelius*) Visits the wilder shores. Will fly upside down for a lark.

NB *Davidus davisus is very rarely sighted.*